MEDICAL DETECTION DOGS

by Megan Cooley Peterson

Consultant: Mark Ruefenacht
Founder and President, Dogs 4 Diabetics

Minneapolis, Minnesota

Photo credits: Cover, ©Leon Neal/Staff/Getty Images; 2, ©Matt Benoit/Shutterstock; 3, ©pfluegler-photo/Shutterstock; 4, ©Phil Date/Shutterstock; 5, ©BJI/Blue Jean Images/Getty Images; 6, ©absolutimages/Shutterstock; 7, ©Michael McGurk/Alamy; 8, ©wavebreakmedia/Shutterstock; 9, ©Joe Giddens - PA Images/Getty Images; 10, ©David Parker/Alamy; 11, ©picture alliance/Getty; 12, ©David Parker/Alamy; 13, ©Bob Pepping/ZUMA Press/Newscom; 14, ©AFP/Pool/Getty Images; 15, ©amandafoundation.org/Getty Images; 16, ©Vitaly Titov/Shutterstock; 17, ©Karl-Josef Hildenbrand/dpa/picture-alliance/Newscom; 18, ©Galka/Shutterstock; 18, ©Sergey kamenskykh/Shutterstock; 19, ©Jessica Hill/AP Images; 20, ©REUTERS/Matthew Childs/Alamy; 21, ©Chris Jackson/Staff/Getty Images; 22, ©The Washington Post/Getty Images; 23, ©Erik Lam/Shutterstock

President: Jen Jenson
Director of Product Development: Spencer Brinker
Senior Editor: Allison Juda
Associate Editor: Charly Haley
Designer: Colin O'Dea

Library of Congress Cataloging-in-Publication Data

Names: Peterson, Megan Cooley, author.
Title: Medical detection dogs / Megan Cooley Peterson.
Description: Minneapolis, Minnesota : Bearport Publishing Company, [2021] | Series: Heroic dogs | Includes bibliographical references and index.
Identifiers: LCCN 2021003697 (print) | LCCN 2021003698 (ebook) | ISBN 9781636911144 (library binding) | ISBN 9781636911236 (paperback) | ISBN 9781636911328 (ebook)
Subjects: LCSH: Animals as aids for people with disabilities--Juvenile literature. | Epileptics--Treatment--Juvenile literature. | Dogs--Therapeutic use--Juvenile literature.
Classification: LCC HV1569.6 .P48 2021 (print) | LCC HV1569.6 (ebook) | DDC 362.17/7--dc23
LC record available at https://lccn.loc.gov/2021003697
LC ebook record available at https://lccn.loc.gov/2021003698

Copyright ©2022 Bearport Publishing Company. All rights reserved. No part of this publication may be reproduced in whole or in part, stored in any retrieval system, or transmitted in any form or by any means, electronic, mechanical, photocopying, recording, or otherwise, without written permission from the publisher.

For more information, write to Bearport Publishing, 5357 Penn Avenue South, Minneapolis, MN 55419. Printed in the United States of America.

Contents

More than a Friend 4
Following the Nose 6
Best Breeds 8
What's That Smell? 10
Getting in Gear 12
All about Alerts 14
Stopping Trouble in Its Tracks 16
Don't Eat That! 18
Cancer-Sniffing Dogs 20

Meet a Real Medical Detection Dog 22
Glossary 23
Index 24
Read More 24
Learn More Online 24
About the Author 24

More than a Friend

The park is full of families and their pets. But for one young girl with **epilepsy**, the fluffy dog running beside her is more than a furry friend. It's her **detection** dog.

Suddenly, the dog smells that something is wrong with the girl. It helps her sit down so she can stay safe. The dog doesn't leave her side. It's a four-legged hero in action!

Medical detection dogs always stay near their owners. They are allowed to go anywhere their person goes.

Following the Nose

Medical detection dogs are working dogs that can sniff out **diseases**. Sometimes, these detectives find diseases that people didn't know they have. This helps doctors treat people before they get sick. Other detection dogs work with people who have diseases that can suddenly get worse. They smell for changes in people's bodies that mean changes in their health, too.

Humans have about 10 million **scent receptors** in their noses. Dogs have up to 300 million!

Medical detection dogs must stay calm while they're on the job.

Best Breeds

What kinds of dogs make the best detection dogs? Any dog with a great sense of smell can train for this important job. But some **breeds**, such as Labrador retrievers and golden retrievers, often make very good medical detection dogs. They are super sniffers and usually work well with people.

When choosing detection dogs, trainers look for dogs that bond well with people. These dogs will be able notice changes in their people's health.

Labrador retrievers are one of the most common breeds of medical detection dogs. They are also the most popular dog breed among pet owners in America!

What's That Smell?

Training to become a medical detection dog begins with the nose. The dogs learn to recognize the smells needed for different jobs. Some dogs learn the scent of a healthy person's body so they can notice when the person becomes sick. Other dogs learn what **cancer** smells like or how to smell a food that could make a person sick.

Each medical detection dog trains for one job, such as sniffing for cancer or a certain disease. They train by sniffing samples of these things to learn what they smell like.

A medical detection dog will practice smelling a disease over and over until it learns the scent.

Getting in Gear

Medical detection dogs may also need to train with special gear. These furry helpers often wear vests to show people that they are working dogs. Some detection dogs also wear a piece of fabric called a bringsel (BRING-sul) on their collars. When a dog smells that its person is about to become sick, it is trained to hold the bringsel in its mouth. This lets the person know to get help right away.

Always ask before you pet a medical detection dog. The dog is working and needs to be able to pay attention to its job.

Medical detection dogs practice passing the bringsel to their person so they can be ready to use the tool if they need it.

All about Alerts

A bringsel is one way a detection dog learns to tell its person that something is wrong. But the dogs are also trained to warn people in other ways. A detection dog might stare at its person, nudge its person with its paw or nose, or lie down. These signs are all different kinds of **alerts**.

Medical detection dogs and their owners are always together.

Medical detection dogs get to know their people's normal smells so they can learn what it smells like if something is wrong.

Much of medical detection dog training happens after dogs are paired with their owners. The humans and dogs get to know each other and work together as a team.

Stopping Trouble in Its Tracks

Some detection dogs work with people who have diseases. People with epilepsy have **seizures** that can make them shake or freeze up. A seizure detection dog can smell when a seizure is coming and alert its owner. The dog will then help make sure its person is safe.

A seizure alert dog can be trained to fetch a phone or find other people. That way, its owner can get more help.

Diabetes detection dogs may be able to bring their owners medical supplies.

Other dogs are paired up with people who have **diabetes**. These detection dogs can smell when blood sugar levels change too quickly. Then, they alert their owners in time for them to get the help they need.

Don't Eat That!

Some detection dogs have the job of sniffing for food! Some people are **allergic** to different foods, such as peanuts. Eating or touching these foods can make them very sick. Allergy detection dogs are trained to smell for these problem foods near their people. These dog detectives are heroes keeping people with allergies safe from harm.

Allergy detection dogs sniff everything their people might come in contact with, including other people or furniture.

Allergy detection dogs can help people of any age.

Cancer-Sniffing Dogs

Many detection dogs work only with their owners. But cancer-sniffing dogs work with many different people. These special dogs learn the scents of the spit, pee, and breath of people who have cancer. Then, they can smell the illness in other people.

Cancer-sniffing dogs are very good at finding the disease. In one study, they were successful more than 98 percent of the time!

Most medical detection dogs work until they are about 10 years old.

No matter how they do their jobs, medical detection dogs are heroes. They help keep people safe from harm day and night.

Meet a Real Medical Detection Dog

With her large eyes and curly fur, goldendoodle Mindy is a pretty cute sidekick. But for Evan, she's more than that. Evan has epilepsy and Mindy is his detection dog. She stays by Evan's side at all times. If he's about to have a seizure, Mindy starts licking Evan. She also barks to alert others about what is happening. Mindy is the hero that keeps Evan safe.

Evan and his family traveled all the way from Virginia to Ohio to train with Mindy before taking her home.

Glossary

alerts behaviors used to bring something to a person's attention

allergic having a condition that causes a person's body to react badly to something

breeds groups of dogs that look and act in a similar way

cancer a disease that destroys parts of the body

detection finding or discovering something

diabetes a disease in which a person's body cannot control the amount of sugar in their blood

diseases illnesses

epilepsy a brain disease that can cause seizures

medical something that has to do with medicine

scent receptors cells in the nose that are used for smelling

seizures sudden attacks that can cause a person to shake and lose consciousness

Index

allergies 18–19
breeds 8–9
bringsel 12–14
cancer 10, 20
diabetes 17
diseases 6, 10–11, 16, 20
epilepsy 4, 16, 20
gear 12
owners 4, 9, 14–17, 20
seizures 16, 22
training 8, 10, 12, 14, 16, 18, 22
vests 12

Read More

Jones, Dale. *Service Dogs (Heroic Dogs)*. Minneapolis: Bearport Publishing, 2022.

Laughlin, Kara L. *Seizure-Alert Dogs (Dogs with Jobs)*. New York: AV2 by Weigl, 2019.

Learn More Online

1. Go to **www.factsurfer.com**
2. Enter "**Medical Detection Dogs**" into the search box.
3. Click on the cover of this book to see a list of websites.

About the Author

Megan Cooley Peterson is an author and editor. She grew up with two lovable dogs—a German shepherd named Sheba and a golden retriever named Gus. She lives in Minnesota with her husband and daughter.